The 'Silver Lady' – sometimes known as the 'White Lady' – London Transport Routemaster RM664, WLT 664, which went into service in 1961 in an experimental unpainted livery. In original condition, it is seen as it first ran on route 276 between Streatham and Tottenham, with a lady showing why we now have 'low-floor' buses.

The idea was that it saved the cost of painting the vehicle, as well as a small saving on the unladen weight of the vehicle. A number of other buses were run unpainted around the country for a while, in Liverpool, Edinburgh, South Wales and elsewhere, but the experiments were not continued, the buses gaining fleet livery after a few years. It was a different story with London Underground trains, however. *(aaq557)*

KEY

Vinta...

Editor: Mike Forbes
Designer: Debbie Walker
Managing Director: Adrian Cox
Commercial Director: Ann Saundry
Marketing Manager: Martin Steele

First Published: March 2014

ISBN: 9780946219568

Published by
Key Publishing Ltd
PO Box 100, Stamford,
Lincolnshire PE9 1XP

© Key Publishing 2014

Visit the Key Publishing website at:
www.keypublishing.com

Printed in England by:
Precision Colour Printing Ltd, Telford.

Vintage
ROADSCENE

www.roadscene.com

Vintage Bus & Coach

Welcome to Vintage Bus and Coach, the first in a series of special souvenir collectable books, illustrating the glorious heritage of bus and coach transport. With unrivalled access to the 'Stilltime' collection of pictures owned by Chris Hodge Commercials, it offers a wonderful celebration of these marvellous old passenger vehicles.

Within the book, I have tried to cover as wide a range of subjects as possible, with sets of pictures from different eras, showing the vehicles of Tilling, BET, municipal and independent operators, featuring both buses and coaches, with well-known types alongside much rarer birds, including as much information as I can about the vehicles and operators, given all the usual limitations. In each category, there are many more sets of pictures for use in the future as well.

The pictures in this book of the AEC Regal IV prototype are timely, as the vehicle has just been re-launched by the London Bus Preservation Trust, following a lengthy restoration. Central SMT was one of the less glamorous Scottish Bus Group companies, running an interesting mix of vehicles. The pictures of Hicks of Braintree, just before the company was nationalised and taken over by Eastern National, are fascinating.

Leyland's experimentation in the 1950s with rear-engined buses, which was to have such far-reaching consequences, makes another interesting subject, while London Transport's much-maligned AEC Merlin single-deckers have passed into history in a manner quite different from the almost contemporary Routemasters.

Meanwhile, Midland Red remains something of a mystery to many enthusiasts, in spite of the sheer size of the company and its vast operating area, not to mention its 'home-made' vehicles, which showed the way for many other manufacturers and operators. At the other end of the scale, a name which lived on for many years was Salopia, a company which an a particularly varied fleet in the early post-war years, offering an intriguing set of pictures.

Southdown is a name which is widely known and loved. Again, its individualistic vehicle specifications make for interesting pictures. A visit to the North-east, where company and independent operators rubbed shoulders in what seemed to be excellent bus territory, is another 'must'.

Then there are some historic pictures of Victoria Coach Station, for many years something of a Mecca for coach enthusiasts especially, and a riot of colour – not entirely lost in black and white – while we round off with pictures of the fleet of perhaps a typical northern municipality, Wigan.

There are many more pictures available in all these different categories, so there is lots to look forward to in further books in the series. If any reader has anything to add or comments to make, please contact me via the publishers and we can use your contribution in a future book or our monthly magazine, Vintage Roadscene, as appropriate.

Mike Forbes is a life-long transport enthusiast and, having spent most of his working years in the road transport industry, is now editor of *Vintage Roadscene* magazine. The pictures in this book come from one of the main archives used in the production of *Vintage Roadscene*, the 'Stilltime' collection of pictures from Chris Hodge Commercials. The reference number of the pictures are included and copies can be purchased via the website www.stilltime.net.

UMP 227 shows off the position of its underfloor engine when it was new. (aat557)

Prototype Reborn

The prototype AEC Regal IV, UMP 227, is well-known to most bus enthusiasts. One of four home market and export prototypes, it was built in 1949 and bodied by Park Royal, initially with 40, later reduced to 38 seats, to the dimensions then in force, 27ft 6ins long by 7ft 6ins wide.

The second home market prototype was later sold to Douglas Corporation in the Isle of Man. One of the two-door 30ft by 8ft export prototypes survived as a café at Hindhead on the A3 into the 1970s.

UMP 227 is now the only known survivor. It was delivered to London Transport, operating from Reigate and St Albans garages, and evaluated against other vehicles supplied by AEC's competitors. It was found more suitable for LT's operations, leading to the order for the RF class as the standard post-war single-decker for London. UMP 227 also acted as a demonstrator to operators in other part of the UK, including Edinburgh Corporation.

Having returned to AEC in 1951, the vehicle was used as a test bed for new equipment, like the Routemaster and Reliance gearbox and Reliance steering system, but never gained power steering. Because of chassis modifications, it retains these, including a semi-automatic overdrive gearbox.

It was subsequently used as a works hack, most of the seats were removed and a workbench fitted and tools and welding gear carried in conjunction with on-going development work. It was first painted overall grey, then AEC's works colours of yellow and blue.

It remained with AEC until bought by the late Alan Allmey in 1971. It was repainted green and white, but damaged by vandals. After Alan died in a dreadful accident in 1978, his brother Donald took on the role of safe-keeping of UMP 227.

Partially repaired, in 1986 it passed to Ian Barratt, who carried on with the restoration, but it spent many years in a corner at the old Cobham Bus Museum. Members of the London Bus Preservation Trust bought the bus in 2008 and a team began restoration in earnest, using photographs, drawings and sacks and boxes of components.

There was much work to do, inside and out, from rebuilding the steps, door mechanism, re-panelling, re-profiling the distinctive front, inner and outer mudguards, ceiling vents, luggage racks, windows and particularly the seats, which had to be made up with new steel balls on the tops of the frames. Repainting to its original livery was not without problems, but has been completed.

After five years, the fully-restored UMP 227 was triumphantly presented to the public at LBPT's 'Transportfest' in October 2013.

These pictures were taken when the AEC Regal IV prototype, UMP 227, was new and being shown to London Transport. The styling of the Park Royal body was a curious blend of old-fashioned and up-to-date features. *(aat 559)*

EMERGENCY EXIT ONLY

Vintage Bus & Coach

Left and above: Interior views looking forward and backward inside UMP 227 show the London Transport-style moquette and those distinctive balls on the seat frames. The forward view reveals a pre-war RT, STL and an RTL in the background. *(aat558/560)*

Scottish Sojourn

When Commercial Motor and the other transport press went to Glasgow, to cover the Scottish commercial vehicle show, then at Kelvin Hall, they would also visit different operators while there, putting together biennial 'Scottish Special' issues.

On one occasion in the late 1950s, Central SMT was favoured with such a visit, resulting in the pictures seen here. Central was part of the Scottish Bus Group, the nationalised provider of bus services north of the border. Unlike the English nationalised companies, however, the SBG operators were allowed to buy other makes alongside Bristols.

Central SMT covered two distinct areas, to the north-west of Glasgow, serving western Dunbartonshire, and to the south-east, serving most of Lanarkshire. Here, a number of centres of population in central Scotland, including Motherwell, Hamilton, East Kilbride, Wishaw and Airdrie, meant that Central SMT's services were mainly urban and comparatively intensive.

Unfortunately, the company has effectively disappeared since deregulation and privatisation of SBG, so these views are but a memory of glories past.

Here is Northern Counties lowbridge-bodied Leyland Titan PD3, no L593, GM 8833, passing an old-style road sign and Kingsway in East Kilbride, heading towards Whitemoss. Central SMT took several batches of Leyland Titan PD2s alongside the Bristols during the 1950s and early '60s. It bought 10 of these PD3s in 1957 with eight more seats than the PD2s but bought no more 30ft double-deckers until 1962. (aat669)

A rainy Castle Street in Hamilton, with an early Bristol Lodekka LD6G, fleet no B45, GM 7645, turning into Cadzow Street, past Skelton's Bar. The vehicle was new in 1956 and has an earlier style destination screen and an open platform. *(aat667)*

Vintage Bus & Coach

During World War II, when the preferred Leylands were not available, Central SMT took Brush lowbridge Utility-bodied Guy Arab IIs. From the first batch, delivered in 1943, H5, BVD 88, its gasket-mounted glazing showing a dgree of rebuilding, is seen turning from Hamilton Road, Motherwell, into West Hamilton Street, heading for Wishaw. *(aat673)*

Left: Strachans-bodied Guy Arab II, fleet no H37, BVD 737, dating from 1946, heads for New Stevenston on service 43. It also shows signs of rebuilding, unlike earlier H22, BVD 242, seen behind, with all-Leyland PD2, L478, GM 5878, on route 93 to Motherwell. *(aat672)*

This page: An Alexander-bodied PD2, L575, GM 8815, is caught near Motherwell Town Hall in Hamilton Road, on service 67 to Newmains. *(aat674)*

Offering a direct comparison between the Leylands and Bristols in the Central SMT fleet, here is Northern Counties-bodied PD2/20, L503, GM 7703, passing LD6G, B93, GM 9993, at Motherwell Cross in Hamilton Road, Motherwell, heading from Glasgow to Newmains and Strathaven to Airdrie respectively. *(aat677)*

Earlier Leyland PD2, with Leyland lowbridge body, L432, DVD 290, in Hamilton Road, Motherwell, nears its destination of Motherwell Cross. *(aat679)*

Farther up Castle Street, Hamilton, with Skelton's Bar and a Lodekka visible in the distance, an inspector talks to the driver of Guy Arab III, K29, GVD 29, with Guy-built 33-seat single-deck body. One of the last of its type built, it looks most old-fashioned. A similar vehicle, K24, EVA 324 of 1950 is preserved. *(aat680)*

Leyland PD2/Alexander L530, GM 7730 passes the National Commercial Bank of Scotland in Cadzow Street, Hamilton, on route 56 to Shotts. Along with the later Bristol Lodekkas, this had the later SBG style of destination indicator. *(aat681)*

Independent Strength - *but not for long*

Hicks Brothers was a local bus company based in Braintree, in northern Essex. It was nationalised and taken over by Eastern National Omnibus Company in 1949. There was a lot of opposition to nationalisation from some operators, led in Essex by Moores of Kelvedon, which held out until the early 1960s.

A number of the Hicks vehicles remained in use in the ENOC fleet for some years, while Hicks was run as a separate business until 1955, when it was wound up and the vehicles were transferred to the main fleet. These included Leyland PD1/ Leyland L27/26R, MNO 193/4, which were new in 1947, as Hicks fleet nos 81/82, later becoming ENOC 1115/6, with 1116 at least losing its roof in 1961, to become PO33/26R.

The takeover by ENOC in 1949 included Hicks' garage, which had been opened in 1922, plus the company's Silver End depot, taken over in the early 1930s from Crittall, along with its Leyland TS1 buses.

A well-known former Hicks vehicle, which is now preserved is 1929 Leyland Titan TD1, L27/24RO, WH 1553, now back in its original Bolton livery as fleet no 54. Four buses, WH 1551-4, were sold to Hicks in 1936. It is believed that the ex-Bolton vehicles were rebuilt with enclosed staircases while with Hicks. WH 1553 retained its petrol engine, being sold in 1947 to Honeywood, of Stanstead, Suffolk, taken over by Goldsmiths of Sicklesmere, and passed back to Leyland in 1958 for preservation. The others were fitted with Gardner diesels, with 1551/2 remaining in service until 1952.

The Hicks Bros livery was mid-blue, with pale yellow relief. Most, if not all the vehicles were Leylands from the 1920s, varying from PLSC1 Lion to Titan PD1. The company had its own workshops and undertook extensive rebuilding and re-bodying.

The full story can be found in Hicks Bros Ltd, An Essex Bus Company, by Anthony Langley of Wethersfield, Braintree, published in 1991 - if you can find a copy.

The pictures here date from a visit by Commercial Motor to the Hicks operation at Braintree not long before the company was nationalised, probably in connection with the anti-nationalisation campaign. A number of the double-deckers pictures carry a 'British Buses' logo, which it is suggested was one of the organisations opposing nationalisation.

Here we see Braintree bus station, provided by Braintree & Bocking UDC, apparently now the site of a supermarket, with Hicks fleet no 65, HF6705, a 1931 Leyland Titan TD1, originally Wallasey no 59, with an Eastwood & Kenning H27/21D body. This had a 'piano front' and an exit with folding doors at the front nearside, but looks to have been heavily rebuilt since acquisition by Hicks in 1939. It looks rather down at heel, with its painted radiator askew. Its departure for Chelmsford in front of the horse and cart, in those more leisurely days, doesn't seem to be of as much interest to the cart driver as the photographer. There are another two of Hicks early 1930s Leyland 'deckers in the bus station, along with Eastern National Bedford OB coach, LPU 624, which appears to be carrying a number of service personnel among its passengers. *(aat870)*

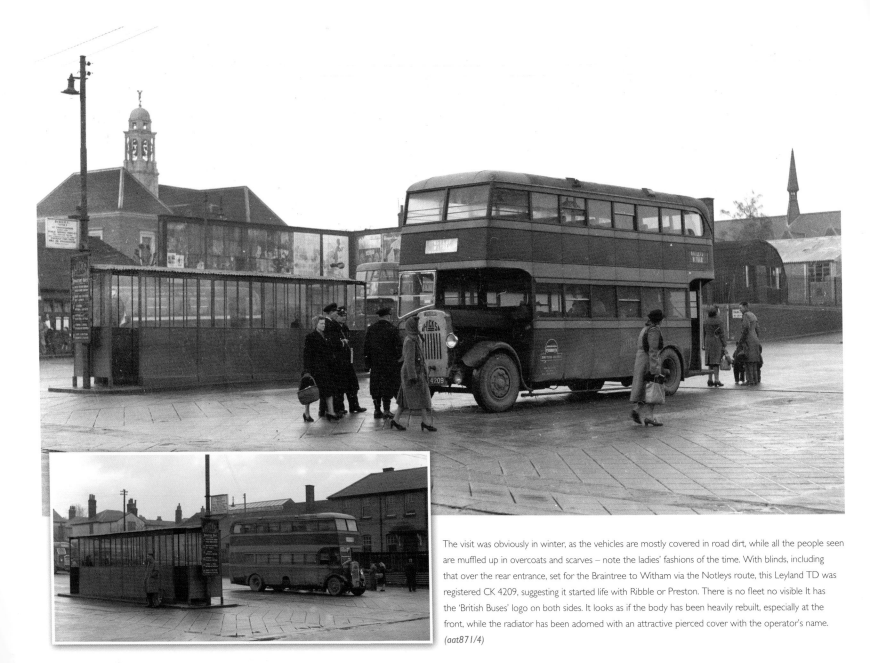

The visit was obviously in winter, as the vehicles are mostly covered in road dirt, while all the people seen are muffled up in overcoats and scarves – note the ladies' fashions of the time. With blinds, including that over the rear entrance, set for the Braintree to Witham via the Notleys route, this Leyland TD was registered CK 4209, suggesting it started life with Ribble or Preston. There is no fleet no visible It has the 'British Buses' logo on both sides. It looks as if the body has been heavily rebuilt, especially at the front, while the radiator has been adorned with an attractive pierced cover with the operator's name. (aat871/4)

Here we have the Hicks Bros garage; notice the timetable case to the side of the door. The vehicles are Leyland TD1, fleet no 50, WH 810, delivered to Bolton in 1928 with an outside staircase body, but now enclosed, and single-deck Leyland Lion, fleet no 41, with Essex registration, BTW 374, awaiting their next duties. *(aat 873)*

Two more single-deckers seen outside the depot were VX 5662 and TF 6615, a Lion LT2 from 1931, which apparently remained in service until 1956. *(aat872)*

Eastern National also ran services from the Braintree bus station. At the time, its fleet also contained plenty of older vehicles, like this early AEC Regent, fleet no 3024, registered TM 6302, probably now with a Gardner engine and re-bodied with a with a semi-Utility body. *(aat876)*

Another vehicle seen on the Chelmsford service, which was obviously well-patronised in those days, was then nearly new Leyland Titan PD1, fleet no 81, MNO 193, seen here setting off from the centre of Braintree. This vehicle remained in the ENOC fleet long after the takeover. *(aat879)*

CHELMSFORD

81

LEYLAND

MNO 193

BUS STOP

Seen inside the depot were these three buses, one of the ex-Bolton TD1s, fleet no 51, WH 1551, its front end rebuilt with a new radiator adorned with the Hicks slatted cover; fleet no 58, CHK 788, a pre-war Dennis Mace, which was probably originally in the Eastern National fleet; and fleet no 43, GNO 579, a Leyland Lion single-decker. It is interesting that most of the single-deckers appear to have been bought new, while the majority of the double-deckers were second-hand, having had a short life with their original operators pre-war. *(aav607)*

The Hicks Bros workshops took on extensive rebuilding of vehicles, as demonstrated by the bare chassis seen here, while the attention to the bodywork and livery of the fleet (left) was, in the main, first class. *(aav606/aat880)*

The Leyland Lion single-decker, fleet no 41, BTW 374, is seen here in the centre of town. The bus, complete with roof luggage rack, is still in good condition, despite its advancing years and the depravations of wartime operations. The chap standing casually in the doorway looks to be wearing a busman's coat, but you can just make out what looks like the conductress, also eyeing the photographer. *(aav609)*

Now for something completely different
or then again, perhaps not...

Leyland was at the forefront of putting the engine at the rear of double-deckers during the 1950s. The company built two experimental 'Low Loaders', STF 90 and XTC 684, which led surprisingly long lives, latterly with independents, after being shown to operators to assess their interest in the concept.

These first two prototypes had their engines across the rear and, in spite of STF 90 being full-fronted, they both had rear entrances. They were built to the current maximum dimensions at the time, 27ft long and 8ft wide, but when the length limit was increased to 30ft in 1956, the way was open for the prototype Atlantean, 281 ATC, to have a set-back front axle, allowing an entrance alongside the driver.

Although one-man-operation was still well into the future, this could be said to be the start of the revolution. The Atlantean prototype was never sold to an operator, unlike the Low Loaders, having a few features which did not go into production, like the wrap-around driver's screen. However, events were moving along quite fast and, by 1958-9, production Atlanteans were entering several fleets not necessarily known previously for their forward thinking.

The front-engine, rear-entrance double-decker fought a long rear-guard action with many operators, but the writing was on the wall, whether we as enthusiasts liked it or not.

Here is the first prototype Saunders Roe-bodied Leyland 'Low Loader', STF 90, which appeared in 1954, two years before the Atlantean, the development of which it led to. Seen at that year's Earls Court show, the bus had its engine, originally a Leyland O.350, under the stairs on the rear open platform. It was one of the vehicles displayed outside, which took interested parties for a run, and seems to be getting a lot of interest from all the people around it. *(aaq310)*

Vintage Bus & Coach

Left: The Low Loader sets off for one of its demonstration runs, carrying a number of passengers. The rear entrance layout was not continued after this and the second Lowloader prototype, although they both went on to give relatively long service lives after their experimental days were completed. apart from the rear-mounted engine and full-front, this vehicle had a more or less normal layout. Note the semaphore indicator located behind the driver's side window. *(aaq308)*

Below: The Low Loader lined up with the other Leyland exhibits outside Earls Court. It is between a left hand drive Leyland-MCW Olympic 'El Omnibus Engles' and a Plaxton-bodied Tiger Cub, HHE 200, destined for West Riding operator Roberts, plus an Olympian, an MCW-Leyland product, TPH 996, then a Duple-bodied forward-control Comet 90, plus EBR 202, a Daimler CVG5/Roe, fleet no 202 of Sunderland Corporation. *(aaq312)*

At the 1956 show, the first Atlantean was on display. Here it is seen part-finished in various views at the Metro-Cammell works, showing off various interesting features, like the wrap-around driver's screen, glass-fibre domes, low entrance and overall height, enclosed rear engine in the company of an Edinburgh Orion-bodied Titan and other vehicles, including another export Olympic and some older-looking AEC double-deckers. *(aar174/6/8/9)*

Seen on road test, followed by a Preston Corporation Titan, before its appearance at the 1958 show is the Alexander-bodied Atlantean, destined for the Glasgow fleet, giving us an idea of the progression of the rear-engined Leyland double-decker during the late-1950s. *(aav356)*

The First Red Arrows

The transport press were on hand to cover the introduction of the first Red Arrow services in Central London in April 1966, as it was the subject of much interest, involving as it did so many changes in operating practices at once. The new buses contrasted in many ways with what Londoners were used to.

Not only were the vehicles single-deckers, and maximum length, at 36 feet long, they were also one-man-operated (equal opportunities were only just advancing over the horizon then).

They also took 'crush-loading' to a new level. Many continental bus passengers were already used to 'standee' single-deckers, but these buses with only 25 seats at the rear and space for 48 standing were a new concept in the UK. And, as well as being expected to 'pay as you enter', there were turnstiles at which those with the exact fare could pay.

It was all part of London Transport's 'Reshaping Plan', to meet the needs of moving London's population around, in the face of increasing congestion.

The vehicles involved were XMS 1-6, as they were then known, later to become MB1-6, which had AEC Swift chassis – although the 36ft long versions were known as Merlins by LT – bodied by Strachans, unlike the rest of the LT Swift/Merlin fleet, which were bodied by MCW.

The rear-engined chassis was ideal for the standee concept, allowing the front section to have a low floor – perhaps not as we understand this today, but compared with most buses of the day, single-deckers in particular.

The first Red Arrow service provided an express service between Victoria and Marble Arch at peak-hours, with a shoppers service to the West End during the rest of the day. The buses were based at Gillingham Street (GM) garage near Victoria.

The Swift/Merlin single-deckers were less than successful on other London Transport and London Country services, but the Red Arrow routes prospered, even if the vehicles used changed over time.

The Red Arrow service departed from one of the bays in the congested 'bus station' outside Victoria railway station, further cramped by building work. Here XMS5, JLA 55D, is the centre of attention, as it loads between an RTL and an RM and RT. *(abi446)*

Under the watchful eye of an inspector, passengers board XMS6, JLA 56D, at the new bus stop for the 500 Red Arrow service to Marble Arch. *(abi427)*

Having taken its 'crush load' on board, XMS5 turns into Victoria Street on its journey to Marble Arch, showing off its 'Red Arrow' fleetname and the split windscreen and peaked front dome of its Strachan bodywork. *(abi421)*

Offering a contrast, the Red Arrow is followed out of Victoria by the 'old order', Routemasters RM 1694 and RM1364 on routes 16 ad 36, which will follow much the same route. Both are also well-loaded. *(abi422)*

This rear view of XMS3, JLA 53D, with its advert for the new flat-fare (6d) service, emphasising its 73 passenger carrying capacity, also highlights the cramped conditions at Victoria in 1966, with no barriers at all; imagine that today... *(abi442)*

Nearing the end of the route, XMS6, JLA56D, is seen in Park Lane, with a full load of passengers, including standees. Many people were obviously keen to give the new service a try. *(abi417)*

The after-life. Some buses have enjoyed a second career as staff buses. Here is ex-Leeds fleet no 145, ANW 688, a 1934 AEC Regent with Roe H30/26R body, now no 742 in the fleet of W & C French Ltd, the civil engineering contractors. A similar vehicle is now preserved. *(aav235)*

Aberdeen Coproration fleet no 188, a 1954 Daimler CVG6, fitted with Crossley H32/28R body is seen making its way past the Aberdeen fish docks on route 15, the Kincorth Circular. *(abb420)*

Midland Memories

Midland Red's buses would always stand out in a crowd. In spite of being part of the BET set-up, the company was allowed to 'do it's own thing' and build its own vehicles. Presumably, this was felt by the powers that be to keep the regular vehicle manufacturers on their toes, although all the individual BET operators were given far more autonomy than the nationalised Tilling companies.

The area covered by Midland Red was very large and spread out across the centre of the country, offering some marked contrasts in the places served. Thus, a visit could result in a series of quite varied pictures. There was also plenty of variation among its vehicles.

Some of the views seen here are still quite recognisable today, while others have changed a great deal as, of course, have the vehicles. Hopefully, I have managed to identify the locations, although in some cases it must be admitted to be an educated guess. There are many more Midland Red pictures in the Stilltime archive, so this is a subject we can return to again in the future.

Most of these pictures were taken some time in the late 1950s at various termini around the Midland Red operating area. One interesting feature to notice is that all these buses had a conductor at the time, including all the single-deckers.

Here is a view of the bus station in Stratford-upon-Avon, still in use in recent years, showing Leyland PD2 double-decker LD8, fleet no 4071, SHA 471, on the 518 route to Coventry via Leamington, along with three Stratford Blue double-deckers – also all-Leyland PD2s – including GUE 238 on the Midland Red subsidiary's route to Kineton, and a single decker with a black roof. There is a Leyland Royal Tiger coach from the Black & White fleet to the right, bound for Cheltenham on an Associated Motorways service. *(aaa592)*

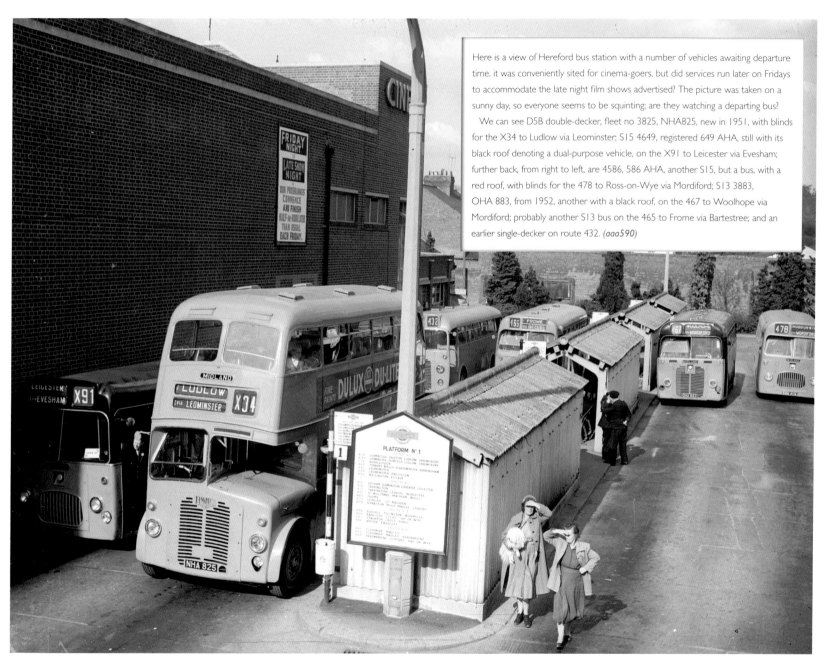

Here is a view of Hereford bus station with a number of vehicles awaiting departure time. it was conveniently sited for cinema-goers, but did services run later on Fridays to accommodate the late night film shows advertised? The picture was taken on a sunny day, so everyone seems to be squinting; are they watching a departing bus?

We can see D5B double-decker, fleet no 3825, NHA825, new in 1951, with blinds for the X34 to Ludlow via Leominster; S15 4649, registered 649 AHA, still with its black roof denoting a dual-purpose vehicle, on the X91 to Leicester via Evesham; further back, from right to left, are 4586, 586 AHA, another S15, but a bus, with a red roof, with blinds for the 478 to Ross-on-Wye via Mordiford; S13 3883, OHA 883, from 1952, another with a black roof, on the 467 to Woolhope via Mordiford; probably another S13 bus on the 465 to Frome via Bartestree; and an earlier single-decker on route 432. *(aaa590)*

This picture was taken in the centre of Hereford, where there are still bus stops. It shows another S15, fleet no 4560, 560 AHA, arriving on the H9 to Hereford via Red Hill. It is passing 3756, NHA 756, an S10 on City Service H16 to Hampton Park, with the crew enjoying the sunshine on layover, in front of double-decker D5B 3807, which is on the City Service to Topsley. *(aaa584)*

A Midland Red C1 coach, ready for departure on a Half Day Tour, outside one of the company's booking and enquiry offices. The boards advertise a Mystery Tour and trips to Bridgnorth, The Cotswolds, the Spalding Tulip Fields and Wicksteed Park. *(aaa597)*

A view inside Stourbridge Garage, where passengers could board buses under cover. On the left is AEC Regent II double-decker, AD2 class, fleet no 3180, JHA 81, on the S53 service to Wollaston Farm via Wollaston and, on the right, one of the GD6 class Guy Arabs, originally Meadows-engined, on the 245 route to Wednesbury via Brierley Hill. The D7 behind the waiting schoolgirls is probably on the same route. *(aaa610)*

50

Left: A wonderful semi-rural Worcestershire scene, believed to be Evesham, with Midland Red vehicles awaiting their next duties. From the right, S15, fleet no 4562, 562 AHA, on the 405 service to Pershore via Fladbury – complete with a triangular 'One Man bus' sign in the windscreen; a D7 double-decker, 4530, XHA 530, on service 148 to Birmingham via Bidford-on-Avon; S15 4708, 708 BHA, on the 398 to Shipston via Bretforton; and being passed by the Boy Scout on his bike, S14 4294, UHA 294, on local service E1 to Hampton via High Street. *(aaa612)*

Below: A Coventry scene now, with Corporation buses on the right, including Metro-Cammell-bodied Daimler CVG6, SKV 192, while star of the show is LD8, 4001, SHA 401, on route 159 to Birmingham via Stonebridge, in front of LD8, 4065, SHA 465, with its young crew lounging against the front apron, before departing on the X90 to Stratford via Warwick. An older Midland Red single-decker and D7 bring up the rear. *(aaa615)*

A move to Walsall with, on the right, Walsall Corporation fleet no 177, ODH 96, a full-fronted Park Royal-bodied Leyland PD2 on route 6 to Aldridge, alongside a D7, 4146, THA 146, on the 115 to Walsall via Streetley Station, while D5, 3538, MHA 538, is on the 118 to Birmingham New Street via Great Barr. *(aaa619)*

Right: Three of Midland Red's well-known C5 coaches, led by 4802, 802 HHA, are seen at Digbeth Coach Station in Birmingham, about to leave on the London service via the M1 Motorway, along with a number of other companies' vehicles. *(aaa616)*

Below: The Midland Red 176 route was one of the company's 'Coventry Road' routes, which still runs as the 957 under Travel West Midlands today. The 176 route ran between Birmingham and Solihull via Sheldon and here D9, fleet no 4855, 855 KHA, and S14, 4295, UHA 295, are both seen with blinds set for Birmingham via Sheldon at the outer terminus of the route. *(aaa639)*

Salopia Selection

Salopia of Whitchurch in Shropshire was well-known beyond its local area for its coach tours, but the company also operated local services, including schools contracts and stage carriage services.

The company was originally started by Harry Richards in 1915 then, ten years later, he obtained a Santus-bodied Thornycroft, which was the first vehicle operated under the name Salopia Saloon Coaches – which refers to the other popular name for Shropshire, Salop. This also marked the commencement of the tours operation. This grew to a level which required as many

as 22 new Bedford/Duple coaches each year during the 1960s, according to a contemporary Commercial Motor report.

From the 1970s, following the retirement of Harry Richards, the company was owned by Bee-line and then Shearings, but the Salopia saloon coaches name is now dormant, although another comapany Heath Salopia Coaches operates from Wem Industrial Estate, Shrewsbury.

The pictures here date from a visit by Commercial Motor to the company around 1950. They show vehicles from the fleet on a

spacious parking area – presumably the company's base – next to the Raven Inn seen in the background of some of the pictures. There is still a Raven Hotel and truck stop/café at Prees Heath, where the A49 and A41 intersect.

The vehicles show Salopia had an interesting fleet, with a mix of the less common types of vehicles – with a notable absence of Leylands and AECs among the heavyweights.

Perhaps the reason for the visit, as it was an early underfloor-engined type, was fleet number 60, EUJ 792, a Sentinel SB4/40 with Beadle bus bodywork, which was originally a demonstrator for the manufacturer for six months in 1948, then used by Salopia for its local bus services. (abd233)

Right: Here is FAW 993, fleet no 64, one of two Crossley SD42/7 chassis, with C33F bodywork by Metalcraft, new in 1949. The other was FAW 992, fleet no 63. *(abe785)*

Right: At the same time as the Crossleys, Salopia obtained FAW 991, a Foden PVSC6 with C35F body by Metalcraft, as its fleet no 62. The body, however, has a straight waistrail and slightly different rear dome from the Crossleys. *(abe778)*

Seen in front of the Raven Inn was fleet no 58, a Tilling-Stevens K6MA7, registered EUX 908, new in 1949 with a Bellhouse Hartwell C33F coach body, in the classic half-cab style, but slightly different from the other vehicles new at that time. To the right can be seen the rear of the Crossley. (abe779)

SALOPIA PRIVATE

FUJ 221

Something of a classic, even when the photographer visited Salopia's depot, was this mid-1930s Thornycroft Cygnet, fleet no 12, UJ 5240, with its stepped-waistrail coach body. As well as the stylish Salopia Saloon Coaches on the side, the legal lettering gives the company name, H W B Richards, Managing Director & Secretary, Green End, Whitchurch, Salop. Behind is seen another Bedford/Duple OB, FAW532, new in 1949. *(abd 235)*

In this picture, we see the well-appointed workshops of Salopia, with Dennis Lancet, fleet no 53, ENT 581, over the cleverly arranged 'pit', alongside two Crossleys, FAW 992, the other of the 1949 pair and fleet no 66, presumably a later purchase. Yet another Crossley and a Bedford OB are in front at the lower level. *(abd236)*

Above: The shape of things to come, but still not a mainstream chassis, was this Foden PVRF6 with Whitson bodywork, seen at the 1950 Commercial Motor Show. Salopia also had two Foden rear-engined half-deck observation coaches in the early 1950s, registered JAW 334 and HUJ 996. *(aar728)*

Left: The Crossley, Foden, Bedford, Tilling-Stevens and Sentinel seen before individually were also lined up in the yard for this group photograph. *(abd231)*

United and Divided

The North-east of England has always been known as an area with a large number of independent bus operators, as well as the area Tilling and BET concerns and municipalities. When Commercial Motor journalists visited the area, they took pictures of the vehicles of one of the independents, Wilkinsons of Sedgefield, which started stage carriage services from Fishburn and Stockton-on-Tees to Trimdon Grange and Darlington, via Sedgefield. There was later an express service to Blackpool.

The company always had a smart fleet of buses and coaches, usually Leylands, on its routes, plus the usual schools and

other contracts, tours and excursions. Wilkinsons remained independent until 1967 when, following the death of the managing director and an unrelated fatal accident, it sold out to United Automobile Services.

United had once served a large part of Eastern England, but was split up after acquisition by the Tilling group in 1929, when Eastern Counties and Lincolnshire Roadcar were formed. Later, United was nationalised, under the British Transport Commission, Transport Holding Company and finally the National Bus Company.

United Auto's operating area overlapped that of BET's Northern General and many other operators, and in later years, first rationalisation, then deregulation resulted in many changes.

During the period in which these pictures were taken, United was in many ways a typical Tilling company, with a largely Bristol/ECW fleet, although rebuilding and rebodying can make identification of some vehicles difficult. United also controlled a subsidiary called Durham District Services, which brought together a number of smaller companies nationalised in 1950, to which various different vehicles were transferred over the years.

A lovely line-up of 1950s coaches in the Wilkinsons of Sedgefield fleet. From the left they are fleet no 39, MPT 39, one of the first Leyland Royal Tiger production models, new in 1951 with Burlingham Seagull C39C bodywork; then no 45, OUP 45, another Royal Tiger, new in 1953 with the last of Leyland's own coach bodies; then a third Royal Tiger, no 40, DHL 808, suggesting it was new to a West Riding company, with what looks like Duple Ambassador bodywork; then there are two Leyland Tiger Cubs – the lighter chassis which followed the Royal Tiger, again with Burlingham Seagull bodies, nos 46 and 47, RPT 270 and 271; and finally, looking most out-dated in spite of only being something like five or six years old, a Tiger PS2, no 43, FT 7080. A classic front-line coach fleet for its day. (aar373)

Vintage Bus & Coach

Left: Another view of Wilkinsons two Leyland Tiger Cubs, fleet nos 46 and 46, showing off their Burlingham Seagull bodywork to good advantage; probably the reason for the journalists' visit to the company. *(aar383)*

Right: A nice rear view of one of the new Tiger Cubs, which further emphasises the stylish bodywork. The pedestrian-controlled electric milk cart and the telegraph poles help to date the scene. *(aar386)*

Wilkinsons also ran buses, including some Leyland Tiger Cubs, also bodied by Burlingham, like fleet no 49, TPT 449, seen here heading for Spennymoor, (with driver, conductress and passengers all smiling for the camera) in company with United's fleet no BAL3, GHN 837, a wartime Bristol K6A, rebodied post-war with a standard lowbridge Eastern Coachworks body, but retaining its original high radiator, on a long route to Newcastle, via Durham and Stockton. *(aar376)*

Vintage Bus & Coach

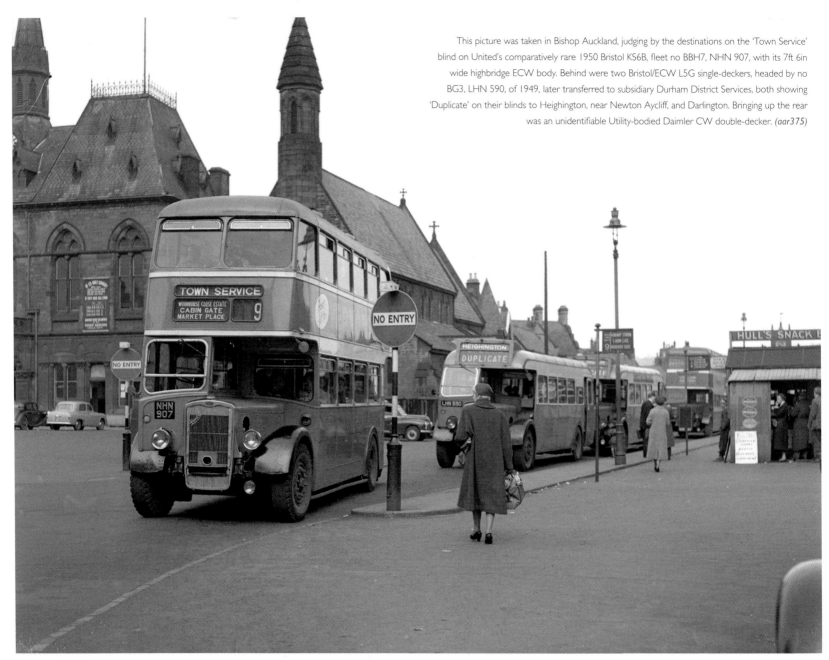

This picture was taken in Bishop Auckland, judging by the destinations on the 'Town Service' blind on United's comparatively rare 1950 Bristol KS6B, fleet no BBH7, NHN 907, with its 7ft 6in wide highbridge ECW body. Behind were two Bristol/ECW L5G single-deckers, headed by no BG3, LHN 590, of 1949, later transferred to subsidiary Durham District Services, both showing 'Duplicate' on their blinds to Heighington, near Newton Aycliff, and Darlington. Bringing up the rear was an unidentifiable Utility-bodied Daimler CW double-decker. *(aar375)*

Here United's Bristol Lodekka LD6B, fleet no BL2, 178 AHN, from 1958, again later with Durham District Services, loads at Barnard Castle, ready to return to Darlington. *(aar 384)*

Vintage Bus & Coach

Left: The next location was High Street, Stockton-on-Tees, where we see two United Auto Bristol/ECW buses, an LS5G single-decker, fleet no BU101, VHN 901, from around 1955, and highbridge KSW6B no BBH52, WHN 52, from the same year, on local Teesside services. *(aar389)*

This page: Another view in Stockton High Street, with another KSW6B, BBH51, VHN 851, to the fore, on the same local service to Roseberry Estate, followed by a Stockton-on-Tees Corporation all-Leyland PD2/3, no 120, JUP 155, from 1949, which is overtaking pre-war Bristol L5G GHN 544 of Durham District Services, with D D S on its dash. *(aar396)*

Vintage Bus & Coach

Above: Moving on to Scarborough, where United had a presence, here was lowbridge Bristol K5G, no BGL62, LHN 305, passing West Square and the Odeon cinema, on its way to Scalby, to the north-west on the edge of the North York Moors. *(aar394)*

Right: Another view in Scarborough, with highbridge Bristol K6B, one of the last built in 1950, fleet no BBH5, NHN 905, on a local service within the town. *(aar402)*

Above: Here we see a Bristol L5G single-decker, no BG474, LHN341, with an ECW dual-purpose body, seen by the extra beading on the sides, but demoted to bus work and livery, making its way across the North York Moors, between Scarborough and Teesside. *(aar401)*

Right: A great shot inside a United depot, at Darlington, judging by the destination indicators, and the Humber Pullman limousine, probably the managing director's car, which would be based at the company's head office. The other vehicles in view include two Bristol L5G single-deckers, BG267, NHN 373, and BG202, GHN 988; an unusual Leyland Royal Tiger PSU1/15, with ECW coach body in the style usually built on the Bristol LS, LUT9, RHN 772, from 1953, in United's lovely coach livery; a lowbridge Bristol KSW6B, BBL73, PHN 823, from 1952; plus two service vehicles, an ex-War Department Canadian Military Pattern (CMP) Ford or Chevrolet box van, on trade plates 022 HN and an early Leyland Tiger TS2, converted to a breakdown tender, on trade plated 055 HN. *(aar400)*

This 1940 Leyland Titan TD7, HF 9126, started life as a H28/26R double-decker with Metro-Cammell body, as fleet no 74 in the Wallasey Corporation fleet. It is seen here, soon after it was converted in 1952, to an incident vehicle for the Lancashire Police. The vehicle was preserved in the 1970s and is still seen at rallies in a red and white livery. *(aac404)*

Victoria victorious

Let us start with a picture from the opening ceremony in March 1932. Police were obviously needed to control the crowds, many wearing bowler hats, as Midland Bus Services fleet no 133, registered VD1433, an oil-engined AEC Regal with Wycombe body, enters with passengers no doubt heading for the opening luncheon. Midland was part of the SMT group and in June 1932 was absorbed into the newly created Western SMT. It was being followed by an Aldershot & District vehicle, with a roof-board for the Farnham-Aldershot-Farnborough-Camberley-Bagshot-London express service. *(abn435)*

Victoria Coach Station was opened in 1932 at its present site in Buckingham Palace Road, by London Coastal Coaches Limited, an association of coach operators, who saw the need for a central location for the arrival and departures of the growing number of express coach services at that time. Victoria has remained the most important coach station in London ever since, despite others, notably at Kings Cross and St Pancras, being used over the years by competing companies.

From 1969, Victoria became part of the National Bus company, but is now owned by Transport for London and still thrives after many expensive improvements as the main terminal for National Express, Eurolines, Oxford Express and Megabus services.

The pictures here date from the opening, later in the 1930s and the early post-war years. Since then, the coach station has grown to have arrivals on the other side of Elizabeth Street and arrangements have to be made for coaches to be parked and serviced elsewhere between trips.

Until the NBC white coach livery swept all before it during the 1970s, Victoria was always packed with coaches in a multitude of different colour schemes, which added to the romance of setting off for all corners of Britain from its departure bays. The pictures here might be in contemporary black and white, but the colourful scenes can be imagined...

Midland fleet no 133 is now seen parked behind a vehicle of Orange Brothers of Bedlington, Northumberland, painted in 'Orange Green', perpetuated in United Automobile's coach livery, after Orange was later taken over, with a roof-board offering a Glasgow-Edinburgh-Newcastle-London service, along with a number of other companies' coaches. The Midland crew stand proudly beside their vehicle wearing their gaiters. A notice on the window offers a Glasgow-London service for 33/- or 50/- return (£1.65 or £2.50). *(abn432)*

Another early view, on a slightly damaged glass plate, with one of Western SMT's early-1930s Leyland Tigers, with 'Coronation Coach' lettering along the roof, behind a Crosville 'Luxury Coach' in the loading bays, as an AEC Regal demonstrator on trade plates 316 H approaches. Notice the stepped waist-rails on the bodies and the steps up to the roof-mounted luggage rack on the Western SMT vehicle. *(aab930)*

A study in 1930s rear ends, with the AEC demonstrator beyond the South Midland coach, fleet no 37, CWL 953, a 1935 Harrington-bodied Leyland Tiger TS7 bound for Oxford, and Southdown no 1087, AUF 787, a Harrington-bodied TS6, later to become a breakdown wagon. Beyond the AEC, it looks like a Crosville coach, then another unidentified but curvaceous vehicle. In the front line, on the right, we have two Maidstone & District vehicles, including fleet no 571, CKO 964, a Harrington-bodied Leyland TS7. Between these and the South Midland coach are Thames Valley no 239, RX 9307, a Brush-bodied Tiger TS4, which appeared at the 1931 Commercial Motor Show, and East Kent JG 6513, a 1935 petrol-engined Leyland Tiger TS7, with Park Royal body, incorporating a roof luggage rack. *(aab925)*

Left: Now we move to some post-war views. Prominent here is a rear three-quarter rear view of Southdown Leyland PS1/1 fleet no 1272, from late 1947, with Windover Huntingdon body, behind another Southdown vehicle, with an Aldershot & District coach glimpsed on the right. To the left are Maistone & District KKK 83x, one of a batch of 55 AEC Regal IIIs, fitted with Harrington coach bodies from earlier vehicles, delivered in 1948-9, one of the East Kent Tiger TS7s from 1935, still in front-line service, then a couple of Bedford/Duple OBs, flanking a Western National vehicle. Over to the left, facing the camera, can be seen an early Royal Blue Leyland Tiger with a Covrad replacement radiator. *(aar319)*

Above: Looking in the other direction, the eye is drawn to the Thames Valley double-decker. Bristol K6B, fleet no 498, EJB 220, with ECW L27/28R body, was operating on Route B to Reading, via Chiswick, Slough and Maidenhead. To the left, we see Bristol fleet no 2152, FHT789, a Bristol L5G from 1939, with Duple C32F body, which left the fleet in 1952, helping to date the photograph. Among the coaches on the right are vehicles from East Kent, Eastern Counties and Maidstone & District. *(aar311)*

Looking down now from the offices, onto the arrivals side of Victoria and vehicles parked awaiting their turn to pull onto the departure bays. Bottom left, we can see two Eastern Counties Bristols, including ECW-bodied JO6A, fleet no LJ468, BVF 118, and four from the Bristol Omnibus Co fleet, three pre-war Duple coach-bodied L5Gs and 1948 dual-purpose DP31R ECW bus shell-bodied L6B, fleet no 2382, KHY 383. In the centre is rather anonymous Duple half-cab bodied FOT 519, with its boot and sliding roof open, behind an equally-anonymous older vehicle, with uniform-less driver, probably an independent's coach hired in on a busy day.

Over in the parking area, we can see, left to right, Southdown fleet no 1289, HUF 289, a 1948 Beadle-bodied PS1, in front of a Maidstone & District coach; then a Royal Blue Bristol L6B with Beadle body, fleet no 1203; another Southdown Tiger PS1/1, fleet no 1259, HCD 859, with East Kent-style Park Royal body from 1947; then two South Midland vehicles, with 1948 Duple-bodied AEC Regal III, fleet no 55, MJO 665, in front; then it is Midland Red fleet no 2270, FHA 402, a Duple-bodied BMMO SON 'ONC', with a blind for Aylesbury and Banbury. Behind and further right, we glimpse two Southdown ECW-bodied Tigers and a Thames Valley double-decker. *(aar321)*

Above: Looking the other way again, we can see the fronts of those newly-arrived vehicles, including Bristol fleet no 2145, a 1939 Bristol L5G, with Duple C32F body, DP31R ECW bus shell-bodied L6B, fleet no 2382, KHY 383 again, three Eastern Counties coaches with ECW C32F, including LJ9, NG 9909, a 1935 Bristol JW, by now fitted with a Gardner engine, but still with its original 'tin bible' indicator, plus what looks like a Southdown ECW-bodied Tiger at the rear. Over in the departure bays, we can see a Maidstone & District vehicle and three Eastern Counties coaches, the rear-most with a roof luggage rack like the M&D coach. Beyond is a glimpse of what looks like a Burlingham-body. *(aar318)*

Finally, a couple of shots which, while not being the best images, convey much of the atmosphere of Victoria Coach Station. Here is a passenger's eye view of some of the departure bays. To the left, we can identify East Kent CFN 61, first of a 1946-48 batch of 50 Park Royal C32F bodied Leyland PS1s, but prominent are three coaches bearing the name Rayners, two Leyland Cheetahs, with Northern Irish registrations CZ 729 and 806 and different style bodies, and a Commer Commando, presumably hired in to cover a busy route. *(aar315)*

Seen threading its way between passengers and East Kent and Maidstone & District Leyland and AEC vehicles, as it leaves the departure bays on its way to Southend-on-Sea, is pre-war Westcliff Bristol J with ECW body, JN 6880, which moved to Eastern National in 1954. *(aar322)*

We all know the Matchbox Toys model of the vehicle, but here is the Leyland Royal Tiger Worldmaster, with that ornate coachwork by Casaro of Turin, at the 1956 commercial vehicle show. It later gained registration number XTJ 885. *(aaq790)*

Leylands in Wigan

Here we have a selection of pictures of buses in the Wigan fleet in the early 1950s. Wigan Corporation Transport was firmly wedded to the Leyland marque for many years, including bodywork while this was still available, right up to 1974, when local government reorganisation took Wigan's fleet into that of Greater Manchester PTE.

In spite of using standard Leyland vehicles, Wigan did have a few idiosyncrasies, like the green lights either side of the front destination indicators, which can be seen in these pictures. These were intended to show potential passengers that it was a Wigan bus approaching, and not one from one of the many other local authority operators which provided overlapping services in the same parts of the Manchester conurbation.

The post-war Wigan Titan double-deckers were also always fitted with a spot or fog light in an unusual position close to the nearside headlamp.

Another unusual feature of Wigan's buses was that the fleet numbers did not necessarily follow the same sequence as the registration numbers as with most fleets. This was doubly strange, as the borough was one which enjoyed its own vehicle licencing authority and registration letters, which tended to make its vehicles look strangely out-dated, even as early as these pictures were taken.

The corporation was lucky to receive a batch of Leyland Titan PD1s soon after World War II. These were to lowbridge layout, while further Titans, PD2s which arrived in 1950, were to highbridge layout. Although waiting until underfloor-engined vehicles became available, Wigan followed the same all-Leyland route with its single-deck purchases as well, with heavyweight Royal Tiger buses in the early 1950s. After Leyland gave up building bus bodies, Wigan turned to other Lancashire-based bodybuilders. None are seen here, as this was after the photographer's visit. All these pictures, taken in a northern industrial town in very wet weather, belie the need felt by many photographers for bright sunny days to get good results.

Left: A classic early post-war street scene, featuring Wigan Corporation fleet no 163, JP 8326, a 1950 all-Leyland PD2 highbridge double-decker, on what was presumably a joint route to Ashton, via Wigan. *(aar428)*

Above: Another of the 30 all-Leyland PD2s delivered in 1950, fleet no 86, JP 8315, is seen in the centre of the town, along with fleet no 18, JP 9061, a Leyland Royal Tiger, this time with Northern Counties bus bodywork. (aar430)

Two more of the large batch of 30 highbridge PD2s delivered in 1950 are seen on the right, facing the camera. The driver of fleet no 85, JP 8319, gives a hand signal as he pulls away, beside fleet no 164, JP 8327. On the left, we see the rear of PD1, fleet no 33, JP 6031, with a lady demonstrating why we have low-floor buses these days, and JP 5535, fleet no 51, both with lowbridge bodywork. (aar434)

Seen in Station Road, where crews obviously changed over at the bus stands, are two more of the lowbridge Titan PD1s, which were delivered in 1946-7. Some like fleet no 21, JP 6027, were graced with a chromium-plated radiator shell, while others, like fleet no 133 JP 5511, had a more utilitarian-looking painted shell. *(aar431)*

Just look at that bus queue. What wouldn't modern day bus operators give for such a sight? Believed to be further along Station Road, here is PD2 fleet no 90, JP 8324, on route 3 to Hindley, obviously a popular destination that day... *(aar416)*

Another view outside the premises of the same 'Automobile Engineers', dealing in Daimler and Lanchester cars, among others, was PD1, fleet no 42, JP 5535, another with a painted radiator shell. The lowbridge layout of the earlier vehicles would have served as a recognition feature, as well as the longer front apron over the offside front wheel-arch. Behind is fleet no 7, JP 3720, a TD3, dating from the pre-war years. *(aar436)*

Above: A view inside Wigan's Central Depot in Melverley Street, showing quite a number of the fleet, presumably in an off-peak period, mainly the older lowbridge examples. *(aar413)*

Right: Wigan fleet no 112, JP 3900, a 1939 all-Leyland TD5, belies its years with its immaculate condition, as it demonstrates the green lights either side of the front indicators. *(aar437)*

Vintage Bus & Coach

Vintage Bus & Coach